P9-DNL-945

HOOPS TO HIPPOS!

True Stories of a Basketball Star on Safari!

Boris Diaw
With Kitson Jazynka

WASHINGTON, D.C.

Staff for This Book
Shelby Alinsky, *Project Editor*
Hillary Leo, *Photo Editor*
Callie Broaddus, *Art Director*
Ruth Ann Thompson, *Designer*
Marfé Ferguson Delano, *Editor*
Paige Towler, *Editorial Assistant*
Sanjida Rashid, *Design Production Assistant*
Colm McKeveny and Michael Cassady, *Rights Clearance Specialists*
Grace Hill, *Managing Editor*
Joan Gossett, *Senior Production Editor*
Lewis R. Bassford, *Production Manager*
George Bounelis, *Manager, Production Services*
Susan Borke, *Legal and Business Affairs*

Published by the National Geographic Society
Gary E. Knell, *President and CEO*
John M. Fahey, *Chairman of the Board*
Melina Gerosa Bellows, *Chief Education Officer*
Declan Moore, *Chief Media Officer*
Hector Sierra, *Senior Vice President and General Manager, Book Division*

Senior Management Team, Kids Publishing and Media Nancy Laties Feresten, *Senior Vice President;* Jennifer Emmett, *Vice President, Editorial Director, Kids Books;* Julie Vosburgh Agnone, *Vice President, Editorial Operations;* Rachel Buchholz, *Editor and Vice President,* NG Kids *magazine;* Michelle Sullivan, *Vice President, Kids Digital;* Eva Absher-Schantz, *Design Director;* Jay Sumner, *Photo Director;* Hannah August, *Marketing Director;* R. Gary Colbert, *Production Director*

Digital Anne McCormack, *Director;* Laura Goertzel, Sara Zeglin, *Producers;* Jed Winer, *Special Projects Assistant;* Emma Rigney, *Creative Producer;* Brian Ford, *Video Producer;* Bianca Bowman, *Assistant Producer;* Natalie Jones, *Senior Product Manager*

The National Geographic Society is one of the world's largest nonprofit scientific and educational organizations. Founded in 1888 to "increase and diffuse geographic knowledge," the Society's mission is to inspire people to care about the planet. It reaches more than 400 million people worldwide each month through its official journal, *National Geographic,* and other magazines; National Geographic Channel; television documentaries; music; radio; films; books; DVDs; maps; exhibitions; live events; school publishing programs; interactive media; and merchandise. National Geographic has funded more than 10,000 scientific research, conservation, and exploration projects and supports an education program promoting geographic literacy.

For more information, please visit nationalgeographic.com, call 1-800-NGS LINE (647-5463), or write to the following address:

National Geographic Society
1145 17th Street N.W.
Washington, D.C. 20036-4688 U.S.A.

Visit us online at nationalgeographic.com/books

For librarians and teachers: ngchildrensbooks.org

National Geographic supports K–12 educators with ELA Common Core Resources. Visit natgeoed.org/commoncore for more information.

More for kids from National Geographic: kids.nationalgeographic.com

For information about special discounts for bulk purchases, please contact National Geographic Books Special Sales: ngspecsales@ngs.org

For rights or permissions inquiries, please contact National Geographic Books Subsidiary Rights: ngbookrights@ngs.org

Trade paperback
ISBN: 978-1-4263-2052-1
Reinforced library edition
ISBN: 978-1-4263-2053-8

Printed in China
15/RRDS/1

Table of CONTENTS

That's me, Boris Diaw. Two of my favorite things are playing hoops and taking photos of wild animals. I photographed these hippos when I was in Africa on safari, a special trip to see wildlife.

HOOPS TO HIPPOS!

I loved watching this little lion cub lounge on a termite mound.

Chapter 1

Hi, my name is Boris Diaw (sounds like DEE-ow). I'm a professional basketball player. I play for the National Basketball Association, or NBA, for short. I play all over the United States. I also play in Europe.

I have played hoops my whole life. I grew up in a small town named Bordeaux (sounds like bore-DOH) in southwest France.

My mom was a pro basketball player, too. She used to shoot hoops with me. The game was her passion. Now it's mine, too.

I love how basketball is a team sport. There's a lot of spirit in it. Everyone on a team must work together. It's like a pride of lions or a pack of African wild dogs.

Animals are another passion of mine. I love spending time outdoors and taking pictures of wild animals. I have taken photographs of wildlife in South Africa, Botswana (sounds like bot-SWAN-uh), Tanzania (sounds like tan-zan-EE-yuh), and India. I've watched hungry lions eat. I've tracked a tigress with her cubs. I have photographed colorful birds, rugged rhinos, and lounging leopards. When I'm at home in San Antonio, Texas, U.S.A., my photos remind me of the peace I feel in the wild.

I started taking pictures of wildlife when I was seven years old. I was on a trip with my mom and my brother, Martin. We had gone to Senegal (sounds like sen-ih-GAWL) to visit my father. Senegal is a small country on the west coast of Africa. My dad still lives there today, in a city named Dakar (sounds like dah-CAR).

Martin and I had never been to Africa before. It was a big adventure for us. Dakar was very different from where we lived. The city smelled musty. The food tasted spicy.

During the trip, I got a disposable camera. I liked taking pictures of Dakar and all the people around me. But what I really wanted to see and photograph were wild animals.

Lion Tracking

Many wildlife lovers on safari hope to see lions. Trackers help find lions by looking for clues in the bush. They look for paw prints or signs of a kill, such as an animal's hide on the ground or bones. They listen for the roar of lions and calls of alarm from animals that lions like to eat. They sniff the air for the sharp smell of lion scat, or poop. Following clues from the bush just might lead to an awesome encounter with a big cat—just don't get too close!

I was excited when we went to camp in the Niokolo-Koba (sounds like NYUH-koh-loh KOH-ba) National Park. My dad told us we'd see wild animals there. It felt like the longest drive ever—eight hours! As we drove deeper into Africa, it got hotter. We weren't far from the Sahara. It was hotter than any place I knew. There were also lots of big, biting flies.

At the wildlife park, we saw hippos, monkeys, and antelope. We saw zebras and giraffes, too. I watched warthogs and their babies. They trotted around with tails held high. We watched and listened to birds, such as parrots and bee-eaters.

Wild animals here seemed different from the animals I loved watching at the zoo in France. In the Niokolo-Koba,

Did You Know?

When it walks, a lion leaves paw prints as long as five inches (13 cm)! Each print has four toe indents, but no claw marks.

I realized that wild animals have lives even when people *aren't* watching.

One night at the park, I started wondering what animals might be watching me. We were staying in little huts with folding beds, but no doors. Earlier that day, I had heard someone say they had spotted fresh lion tracks. *What if a lion looked into our hut?* I thought. *What if it sneaks in?* The idea scared me, but I was excited, too! I kept my eyes open—and my camera ready.

I never did see a lion on that trip. Too soon, we went back to Dakar, back to people and cars and noise. Then my mom, brother, and I flew home to France. But I wanted to go back into the wild. I loved looking at the pictures I took on my trip.

At home, I got back to basketball. I loved it so much, I played all day, every day. I still loved to explore nature, too. Every summer I spent three weeks camping. I built tree houses. I liked being away from the city. I liked hearing only the sounds of wildlife. It reminded me of the wildlife park in Senegal.

When I was a teenager, I went to a boarding school in Paris. Many serious basketball players go to high school there. My life was all about basketball. After high school, I played for a pro basketball club in France for three years. Then in 2003, I got drafted into the NBA and moved to the United States.

While riding in the safari vehicle, we all looked and listened for wild animals. One day, I snapped this shot of a young elephant chasing a baby giraffe.

Chapter 2

SAFARI SIGHTS

After my rookie, or first, year in the NBA, I finally had time to go back to Senegal. I called Martin, and we organized a trip to visit family. I bought a camera at the airport in Paris. It made me think of the camera I had when I was seven. Just like then, I wanted to remember what I did and saw on my trip.

I took pictures of people in Dakar while they waited for buses or crossed the street. The city was so colorful. The wild areas we visited were colorful, too. One day, we visited a place called Lake Retba (sounds like ret-BAH), which is known as the "pink lake." A special bacteria (sounds like back-TEER-ee-uh) growing in the water turns it pink. I took pictures of the lake and the birds. I had fun figuring out how my new camera worked.

A year later, after another season playing in the NBA, I returned to Africa again. But this time, I went to the country of South Africa. I planned to go on a true safari. I wanted to watch wild predators (sounds like PRED-uh-ters) hunt in their natural habitat. I bought better camera equipment.

And I invited my mom to join me.

We went to Kruger National Park. When we got there, the thing that struck me was the peace. No noise, no cars, no nothing. My phone didn't work. I couldn't even get text messages. That was a good thing! It felt like those days as a kid, when I used to go camping.

I usually love to sleep late in the morning. But I was excited about heading out on our morning game drives before dawn. "Game" are the animals you see while driving around a huge park like this one. Our first morning, we drove through the bush in the dark. We rode in a vehicle without a roof or sides. It easily went through tall grass and bushes, and even over small trees. Sticky spiderwebs stuck to my face as we rode along. Branches scraped our arms. We could hear birds squawking and insects buzzing. It was great.

The tracker—the person who looks and listens for signs of animals—sat in a special chair on the hood of the vehicle. He scanned the darkness with a bright light. He kept an eye on the dirt road for tracks. He sniffed the air for fresh poop. I wondered what animals we would see.

The tracker also listened for clues, such as the alarm calls that baboons make when big predators are near. We saw a hyena (sounds like hi-EE-nuh) running along the road. It turned and looked at us with glowing yellow eyes.

At one point, the guide stopped the vehicle. He reached into a low tree.

Did You Know?

A chameleon shoots out its long, sticky tongue to snag an insect, then draws the meal back to its mouth.

When he pulled his arm out, a green chameleon (sounds like kuh-MEEL-yun) clung to his hand. It was cool to see the little reptile's green toes and its big rotating eyes so close up. The guide placed it back on a branch, and we were off again.

After the sun came up, we saw a herd of elephants. The guide turned off the vehicle. We sat there not making a sound. It was like we were part of the herd. We listened as the elephants whispered to one another in rumbles. We watched them shove the tall grass into their mouths with their trunks. I noticed a baby elephant standing in between the legs of his mom. He was so small!

That day, we also watched lions sleeping in the shade. We saw a rhino drinking at a water hole. Lions, rhinos, and elephants are three of the animals in the "big five." These are the five animals people most want to see on safari. The other animals in the big five are leopards and African buffalo. At Kruger National Park, we saw all of the big five.

Though I wasn't a rookie basketball player anymore, I was definitely a rookie photographer. I took lots of pictures. I might take 200 pictures of an elephant eating leaves! Back at the lodge, I would have to sort through hundreds of almost identical pictures. I realized I had to think before I clicked. The mistakes I made helped me learn to be a better photographer.

The “Little Five”

Like me, many people travel to South Africa to see the “big five.” On one of my trips, a safari guide clued me in about the “little five.” They’re also fun to see. They are the:

1. rhinoceros beetle
2. elephant shrew
3. buffalo weaver
4. leopard tortoise
5. ant lion

No matter what animal I saw, big or small, it always fascinated me.

It might look like I stood face-to-face with an African buffalo to get this picture, but I took the photo from a safe distance. These guys can be dangerous!

Chapter 3

FUN AND GAMES

Most of the time on safari, I saw animals from an open vehicle. But sometimes we hiked into the bush on foot. On my own two feet, I felt small, and not as safe as in a vehicle. On the other hand, I could look more carefully at things like flowers and animal tracks, or a shiny dung beetle rolling a ball of zebra poop.

On one of those hikes, a guide

pointed out impala (sounds like im-PAL-uh) droppings. An impala is a kind of antelope. Its poop kind of looks like olive pits. The guide taught us a traditional African bush game. He said it was like a contest where people spit olive pits. It was *like* that game. But in the bush, we didn't spit olive pits. Can you guess what we did spit?

I tried the game. It wasn't that bad! The guide showed me how to pick the right impala dropping. It should be a bit dried up, he told me. I was proud—I didn't win the game, but I did spit my "olive pit" 15 feet (4.6 m)!

On a walking safari, there's no rule against spitting impala poop. But there is a rule against running. A wild animal might attack if you run, because running makes you seem like prey (sounds like PRAY). As a pro athlete, I run every day. But humans are not made to run as fast as wild predators. Humans don't have claws or big teeth, either, but we do have our smarts. It's *not* smart to run near a wild predator.

Another time on a walking safari, as soon as we left the camp, we saw African buffalo tracks. The ranger told us that buffalo are one of the most dangerous animals to run into on foot. They are aggressive, or likely to attack. But we figured they were far away. We kept on walking down a dirt road with high reeds on either side. Suddenly, the ranger stopped.

Did You Know?

Small birds called oxpeckers perch on top of rhinos, giraffes, and African buffalo. The birds "clean" the animals' skin by picking off ticks and other insects.

Warning! Big Horns Ahead

The African buffalo, also called the Cape buffalo, is not an animal to mess with. This large grass-eater can weigh 1,300 pounds (600 kg). That's as much as a large horse. But an African buffalo is much stronger.

African buffalo are very aggressive. They can attack without warning. They protect themselves from lions and other predators—including human hunters—by charging with their thick, sharp horns. When an African buffalo charges, watch out! This big animal can run 30 miles an hour (48 km/h)!

Then I saw the massive head of a male buffalo. He was lying in the tall grass about 15 feet (4.6 m) away from us. I think we woke him up. My heart pounded. The ranger told us to stay together.

Then the reeds started to move as the buffalo stood. Suddenly he was joined by four more buffalo. The five of them looked ready for action, just like a starting lineup in basketball. I could hear their breath. That scared me. We were too close. We carefully walked back, back, back.

Then the buffalo turned away from us and bolted. It sounded like an earthquake. We were so relieved, we just laughed. We walked in the opposite direction. I looked over my shoulder at the buffalo. One of them turned back and looked at me, too.

CLOSE ENCOUNTERS

I was so excited to get this close to elephants. These huge animals can be very quiet. Sometimes my camera makes more noise than they do.

It seemed as if this hyena was staring right at me. Hyenas will eat just about anything they can get their paws on, including fish, birds, and bugs.

Chapter 1

SNEAKY VISITORS

Every time I go on safari in Africa, something unexpected happens. For example, one time in Botswana I was sleeping in a tent when the sound of scratching woke me. I could hear an animal walking around on the other side of the window next to my bed. This was no small squirrel. It was definitely something big.

I wondered if it was a hyena. I had heard hyenas calling to each other earlier that night. They sounded like dogs singing—or like dogs laughing, if dogs laughed.

I thought about grabbing my flashlight and looking out the window. But the only thing between us was a mosquito net. Just one claw into the net, and the animal could get inside the tent. I stayed still, but it was hard to fall back to sleep. The next morning, I saw hyena tracks all around my tent.

Another time, I was with a bunch of friends in Kruger National Park, in South Africa. It was dinnertime at the lodge. Delicious smells came from the kitchen. We couldn't wait to eat.

But we weren't the only ones who thought the food smelled great. I saw something moving in the darkness nearby. At first, I thought it was the lodge manager's dog.

But it was a spotted hyena. It was big and scruffy. The animal looked thirsty and hungry—and sneaky, too. The waiter tried to scare the hyena away. He banged pots with a spoon to make noise. But hyenas don't scare easily. The animal just stood there. Then the waiter threw things at it. Finally, the hyena left.

Later that night, my friends and I were hanging out in the lounge. It was open on the sides. Suddenly, we noticed that the hyena had joined us again.

Two rangers came along to scare the hyena away. They said it was a female. My friends and I nicknamed this hyena "Giselle." Then my friend Eric asked if he could help chase her away. One of the rangers told him, "It's easy. Just make noise and run at her."

But I wondered if it would be that easy. Hyenas can be dangerous. They are scavengers (sounds like SKAV-inj-urs). They eat the leftovers from other predators' meals. But hyenas are also skilled hunters. They can take down big prey.

Eric did what the ranger said. He yelled at the hyena and ran at her. But Giselle just looked at him. It was like she thought he was funny. He tried again, and, eventually, she left. Eric was very proud of himself.

The next night, my friends and I played cards in the lounge after dinner again. We sat around talking with the rangers. Then Giselle came back.

Laughing Hyenas

A lot of people think spotted hyenas are scary-looking. But I think they are very cool. To me, some are even pretty. I admire their bravery and strength. And I'm amazed by all the different noises they make. Hyenas call to each other when they find food—either leftover food from another predator or an animal to hunt. They're also noisy when they fight or play together. Imagine crazy animal noises from a scary movie: growling, grunting, whining, barking, screaming, and giggling. That's what hyenas sound like!

After the night before, Eric thought he knew everything there was to know about scaring off a wild hyena. He told us not to worry. We laughed. But then a few more hyenas crept in behind Giselle. We stopped laughing. The rangers weren't laughing either.

Now Giselle had friends to back her up. Hyenas work together in a pack. Together, they have more power. They gain courage from one another. It's the same as how a basketball team works. You watch out for each other.

Giselle and her friends looked at us in a freaky kind of way, like we were a meal. It was as if they thought, *Mmmm, those humans must taste good.*

I thought about how a hyena's jaws are

Did You Know?

Spotted hyenas may look like large dogs, but they are not part of the dog family. In fact, they are more closely related to cats.

made to crush bones. Even though hyenas are smaller, they have the same jaw strength as lions and tigers.

This time, when one of the rangers tried to chase the hyenas away, they chased him back. I wanted to tell the ranger he was crazy. But then I thought, *He's the ranger. He knows what he's doing.*

The rangers shouted at the hyenas. The kitchen staff banged their pots and pans together. But these hyenas were bold. They slipped into the kitchen, and the cook screamed. The rangers yelled and banged even louder. Finally, the hyenas slunk away into the darkness. And that was the last time Eric chased a hyena!

These hippos looked like they were having a good time together! Hippos spend most of the day in the water, but they come out at night to eat grass.

Chapter 2

TOO CLOSE FOR COMFORT

Being on safari teaches you a lot about respecting the space of others. Giselle the hyena and her friends got a little too close for my comfort. But there have been times when I've gotten too close to an animal's space.

Once we were out on a morning game drive in Kruger National Park when we saw some hippos hanging around in the water. Hippos may look slow and lazy, but they are one of the most dangerous animals in Africa.

Of course, hippos don't eat people. Hippos are herbivores (sounds like HER-buh-vors). They eat grass. But they do attack if they feel threatened. And they can run 25 miles an hour (40 km/h). That's faster than any human being I know.

Since we were near the water, I asked the guide if we could look for crocodiles. The ranger said if we didn't get too close to the water, we could get out of the vehicle and hike along the riverbank. I was happy to keep a safe distance. It was so hot, we figured the crocs and hippos would stay in the water.

We followed the ranger single file. At 6 feet 8 inches (2 m), I'm pretty tall.

But the reeds along the riverbank were taller. I couldn't see very far. I could smell something strong and strange, though. The guide told us it was hippo dung.

Suddenly, I heard grunting and stomping. I couldn't see anything except for the reeds shaking. I didn't know what was out there. Was it charging at me, or running away? My heart pumped like crazy.

Did You Know?

The two tusks in a hippo's lower jaw can grow to be more than one foot (30 cm) long. The animal's jaws are so strong, it can bite a crocodile in half!

Then I saw the huge rear end of a hippo. It was about 15 feet (4.6 m) away. All of a sudden, I felt very small. Luckily, the hippo ran for the water. I was so glad to hear its splash. That was a close call. We were pretty quiet after that happened. Even the ranger didn't say much. I think he was scared, too. We never did see any crocodiles on that hike. But we'd had plenty of adventure for one day.

On another safari, an elephant chased us humans right out of his space. It happened in Botswana. We were on a night game drive and spotted a herd of elephants. We settled in to watch the animals pluck leaves and branches with their giant trunks.

The elephants made very little noise that night. We didn't make much noise either. They hardly seemed to notice the vehicle or us in it. Then a bull,

or adult male, elephant wandered off. We followed him in the vehicle. We thought we were at a safe distance.

But that bull didn't seem to think so. He spun around to face us. He flapped his ears and trumpeted loudly. That meant he was upset. Then he walked toward us—fast! I thought this only happened on TV. I didn't think the elephant would chase us. But he did.

I was worried he could crush our vehicle and us. A large male can weigh as much as two safari vehicles! Our guide tried to drive away fast. The engine roared as he shifted gears. We went faster and faster down the bumpy bush road. The coils in our seats squawked as we bounced. Trees and bushes scraped at us in the open vehicle.

Supersized!

Everything about African elephants is big. Their bodies are big. Their impact on the plants and animals that live around them is big. They are the biggest land animals on Earth. A large male can stand 13 feet (4 m) tall and weigh more than 13,000 pounds (6,000 kg). An adult elephant's trunk stretches to about 7 feet (2 m) long. An elephant's appetite is big, too! An adult can eat as much as 300 pounds (136 kg) a day of grass, leaves, roots, twigs, tree bark, and fruit.

But the elephant kept up. He was speed walking, right behind us, flapping his huge ears. Lucky for us, it was a scare tactic. It was his way of saying, "Get outta here! I don't like you guys near me." We got out of there!

Another time, an elephant stayed in our camp for three days. While he was munching leaves and branches, he blocked the path to the place where our lunch was served. The elephant enjoyed his lunch, but I didn't want to get too close! So I waited to eat. One day, that elephant brought a tree down right onto the gift shop. It put a huge hole in the roof. It was actually kind of funny. That's the beauty of being in nature and the wilderness. I get to see elephants do what elephants do.

Leopards, like this one that I photographed in South Africa, love to hang out on tree branches.

Chapter 3

STUCK IN THE MUD

Every safari adventure teaches me something. For example, being chased by a bull elephant taught me how an elephant says "Scram!" I have also learned that in the wild, things don't happen on my schedule. I have to be patient.

One day on a safari in South Africa, our guide slowed the vehicle. He pointed up into a tree.

I looked up and saw a leopard. Leopards are one of my favorite animals. I love the leopard's beautiful spots and how the big cat is so elegant with its long tail.

This leopard was lounging on a branch, about 20 feet (6 m) up. It had the carcass (sounds like KAR-kus) of a little dik-dik antelope next to it. A leopard will drag its dead prey up into a tree. This keeps it safe from vultures, hyenas, and other scavengers looking for an easy meal.

Did You Know?

Leopards sometimes hunt baboons at night, while the baboons are asleep in trees. Leopards also sometimes catch fish and crabs to eat.

I was so excited! I had never seen a leopard that close in the wild. They are very elusive (sounds like ih-LOO-siv), or hard to find. They usually only come out at night.

I convinced our guide to get closer, so I could get the perfect shot. I wanted to get a picture that looked like the leopard's body and the antelope's head belonged to one animal. I planned to call it the "ante-leopard." But for that angle, we had to get even closer to the tree. The guide moved the vehicle around a bit. That's when we got stuck in the mud.

The guide tried and tried to get the vehicle out, but it wouldn't budge. It felt scary to be stuck with the leopard directly above us, even if it was just resting. Our vehicle had no roof. If the leopard had wanted to jump in with us, it could have.

Leopards sometimes hunt from up in the trees, where their spots help them blend into the leaves. The big cats pounce from above, without warning. But this leopard was just hanging out and chilling. I was glad it had already caught its dinner. We watched it eat a little bit of the dik-dik. We sat very still.

After an hour, the sun started to set. Another safari vehicle finally arrived to tow us out. That's when it got more dangerous. The leopard might have attacked if it thought we were trying to get its food. Every move we made had to be slow, to not startle it. The guides attached a rope to the vehicle and pulled us out. When we got back to the lodge, I was super hungry for dinner.

We went back early the next morning to check on that leopard. It was still there, along with what was left of the dik-dik. The big cat looked up, like it was expecting us.

Spotted Hunters

Leopards are closely related to tigers, lions, and jaguars, but they are smaller. They can weigh up to 176 pounds (80 kg). These beautiful spotted hunters live in parts of Africa and Asia. The leopard's dark spots are called rosettes, because they are shaped kind of like a rose. These spots help the leopard blend in with leafy branches and tall grass. The leopard hunts mainly at night. Slinking quietly through the grass, it stalks prey such as antelope and wild pigs. Then it springs with a deadly pounce!

I got this lucky shot when these African wild dog pups settled down after eating.

WILD ABOUT WILD DOGS

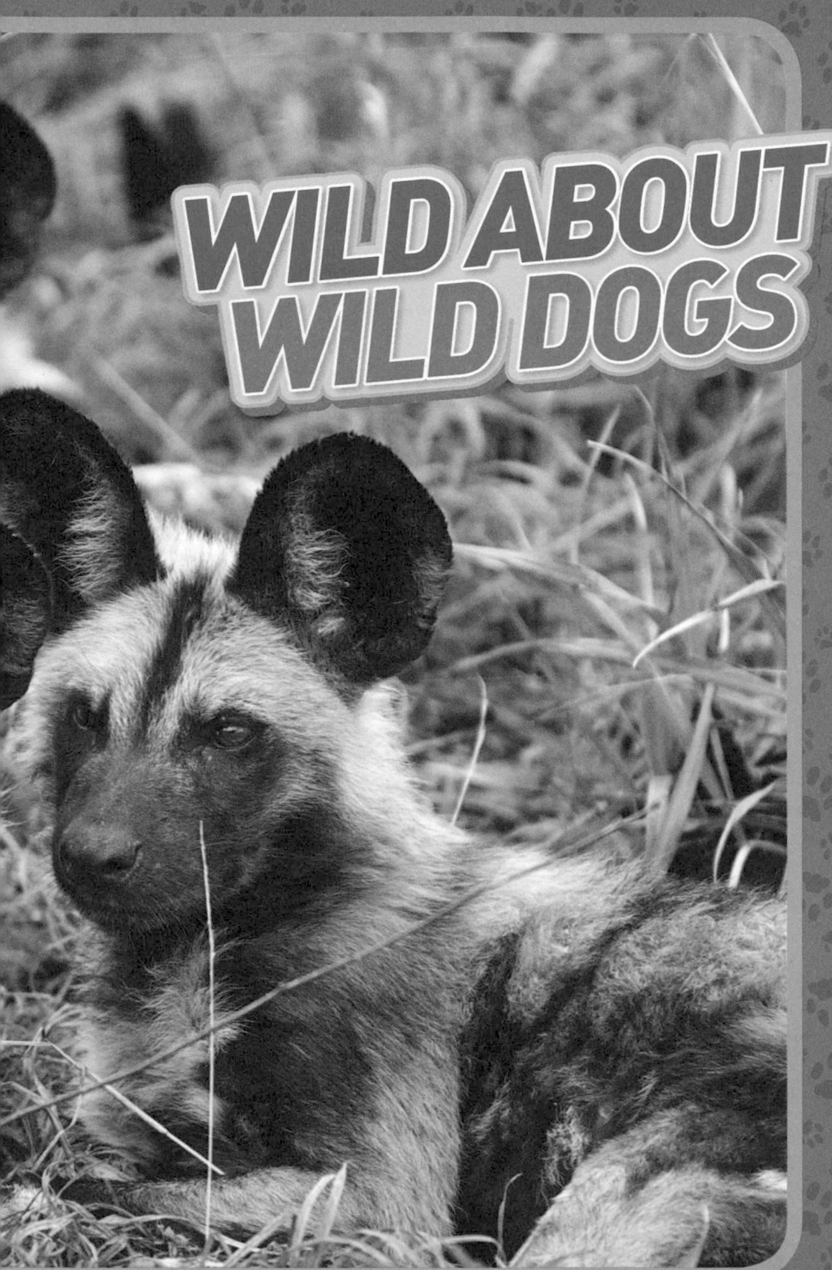

I love coming home to my two dogs at the end of a long day. They're like my own wild "pack."

Chapter 1

TEAMWORK

I have always liked dogs. My brother and I grew up with a German shepherd named Folka. That dog was great. When I didn't want to do my homework, Folka would sit with me. She put my mind at ease. With her next to me, I could focus on my work.

I've got two dogs now. They are Siberian huskies. Croc-Blanc (sounds like CROW-BLAHN) is the male.

His name means "white fang" in French. Neige (sounds like NEJH) is the female. She's all white. Her name means "snow" in French. My dogs are my best friends. It's hard to leave them when I travel. But they're always happy to see me when I come home. I'm happy to see them, too!

When I first heard about African wild dogs, I thought they were homeless pet dogs. After some research, I learned that African wild dogs really are wild. They live in packs. And like a pack of wolves, they take care of each other. Like a team, they hunt together.

Wild dogs used to live all over Africa. But humans have taken over much of their habitat. Now wild dogs have less room to hunt and fewer wild animals to prey on.

So, sometimes, they hunt farm animals, such as goats or cattle. Many wild dogs are killed by people trying to protect their livestock.

Did You Know?

Once, hundreds of thousands of African wild dogs lived in Africa, but today there are only about 5,000 left in the wild.

On my first five safaris, I never saw an African wild dog. So, for my sixth safari, I planned carefully. I went to a game reserve in South Africa known for its roaming packs of wild dogs.

The reserve is near the border of Botswana. I arrived there in the middle of winter. It was really, really cold. Usually on safari I might have to wear a jacket before the sun comes up. But this time I wore a coat the whole time. Being so cold in Africa was a surprise.

One Wild Dog

Both African wild dogs and your family pet dog are members of the group of animals known as canines (sounds like KAY-nines). This group also includes foxes, coyotes, and wolves. All of the 36 members of the canine family are alike in some ways. They all hunt by running down their prey. And they all have excellent senses of smell and hearing. Pet dogs don't have to hunt for food, and they probably love tennis balls more than any African wild dog ever would!

But I was determined to see African wild dogs. One ranger said he thought he knew where some dogs had just had pups. But it wasn't nearby. African wild dogs stay far away from people, especially when they have pups. We would have to go on foot. I pulled on my hiking boots and zipped up my coat.

The ranger said it would be an intense journey. Black rhinos live in this area. Like buffalo and hippos, they can be very aggressive. We walked for about an hour and a half through very thick brush. A lot of the hike was uphill.

Even though I'm a pro athlete, it was a steep hike for me. My camera equipment, including a tripod and a big lens, got pretty heavy. We were almost to the top of the hill, and we still hadn't seen any African wild dogs.

At the top, I looked across the valley. That's when I saw my first ever African wild dog. It was about 650 yards (594 m) away from me. That's pretty far—about the length of 20 NBA basketball courts. The dog trotted up the hill. Then I spotted another one. Then three more!

The African wild dog's scientific name is *Lycaon pictus* (sounds like lie-KAY-on pic-TUS). It means "painted wolf" in Latin. The dogs' splotchy coats do make them look painted. Each wild dog's coat has a unique pattern, just as every zebra has unique stripes, and every human has unique fingerprints.

The ranger used binoculars to watch

the wild dogs across the valley. I looked through my big camera lens to see them closer up. I watched them run, then stop and look over in our direction.

The dogs seemed to be watching us, too. Then they took off, probably to hunt. They disappeared over the side of the hill.

On our game drive that night, we kept an eye out for the dogs. But we didn't see them again. We did see lots of impalas and a pride of lions with cubs. We also saw a family of dwarf mongooses that had made a home in an old log.

I never saw the wild dogs again on that trip. But I left that safari happy. After five years of searching, I had finally seen African wild dogs, even if it was just for two minutes in the distance.

This little guy looks quiet, but baboons are noisy. They bark, scream, and hoot, especially if they sense danger.

Chapter 2

KEEPING UP!

Two years after I saw my first African wild dogs, I went on another safari to celebrate my birthday. I brought some friends along and returned to Kruger National Park in South Africa.

During one game drive, we searched for hippos. On our way to the river, the guide stopped the vehicle so we could watch some baboons near a big marula (sounds like muh-RULE-ah) tree. The fruit of this tree looks like a small peach, but it tastes more like a plum. It's a little bit sweet and a little bit sour. Elephants love this fruit. I tried some once, and I thought it was pretty good, too.

The baboons were sitting around on the ground in pairs. They were grooming each other, not paying any attention to us. We started to leave to move on to the river. But just as we drove off, we heard a commotion behind us. We stopped and turned around to look. The baboons were screaming like crazy and scrambling into the tree. I thought, *Maybe there's a leopard nearby.*

We turned around and drove back toward the tree. I couldn't believe it when I saw two wild dogs run around the tree, sniffing the ground. Wow! We were so close.

The wild dogs' long legs gave them a lanky look, like basketball players. They didn't seem to notice the vehicle or us sitting in it. They were looking around, sniffing the air, smelling the ground, and listening with their large upright ears. They seemed hyper, like they were in hunting mode. Then they ran off, as if someone had called them. We took off after them.

There was no way we could keep up with the dogs, but we tried. They were running and running and running. When they slipped into the bushes, we followed. The safari vehicle strained to get through the thick

Did You Know?

Wild dogs can run as fast as 41 miles an hour (66 km/h) and keep up that speed for up to one hour.

brush. The tracker on the hood of the vehicle kept a lookout.

By the time we finally caught up, a third wild dog had joined the pair. They seemed to have a plan. First, they ran single file. Then they split off in some kind of formation. Were they teaming up to hunt?

One of the dogs held his tail high, like a lead dog would. He seemed dominant. The other two dogs came back to check in with him. They slowed down for a bit to regroup. Maybe they were working out a game plan. Soon a fourth dog joined them, and they all started running again. They yipped and yapped and whined. It was like a relay. The dogs seemed to be taking turns running after the prey.

I didn't know what we were chasing,

but I loved being caught in the middle of the hunt. It felt like I was part of the team. My heart raced right along with theirs.

African wild dogs are one of nature's most efficient (sounds like ih-FISH-unt) predators, thanks to their amazing teamwork. It's like a basketball team: Everyone has a different role, yet everyone works together for a win. Check out the stats: Wild dogs succeed at hunting on four out of five tries. Lions succeed at hunting on only one out of four tries.

Even though the dogs were jogging, not sprinting, it wasn't easy to keep up with them in the vehicle. When we finally caught up with them again, we saw that they had killed a spotted antelope called a bushbuck. They devoured it. They tore it apart with their sharp teeth and gulped it down in chunks.

There's a good reason they were eating so fast. Sometimes leopards, lions, and hyenas try to steal food from wild dogs. So the dogs need to eat fast!

The way the wild dogs hunted and ate was violent, but it's how they survive. It's how they feed their puppies. It was all over in about three minutes.

I felt bad for the bushbuck. But I could appreciate the teamwork and effort the African wild dogs had put into working as a unit. One dog alone could not hunt this well. Teamwork made them powerful. They all respected their positions. And they were all willing to do their part. It's the same on my team.

Appetite for Antelope

Antelope are fast-moving animals that live in Africa and Asia. There are nearly a hundred different kinds of them, and they come in a wide range of sizes. Some are as small as a miniature poodle (dik-diks), and others are as big as a moose (elands). Others are somewhere in between (impalas and bushbucks). An antelope's antlers can be straight, curved, spiraled, or twisted. All antelope have hooves split into two toes. They eat mostly grass and leaves. In Africa, antelope are a favorite meal of lions, leopards, wild dogs, hyenas, and cheetahs.

The day I watched these African wild dogs hunt was one of the best times of all my safari adventures.

Chapter 3

PICTURE PERFECT

Soon after devouring the bushbuck, the African wild dog team—I mean the pack—was on the move again. I guess one kill was not enough food for them.

African wild dogs often hunt smaller antelope, such as gazelles. But sometimes they'll tackle larger antelope, such as wildebeests (sounds like WILL-duh-beasts) or kudus (sounds like COO-dues). The dogs often seek out hurt or weak animals, which are safer to hunt. Hunting can be dangerous. A blow from the hoof of an impala or the slash of a warthog tusk could kill a wild dog.

Wild dogs also snack on birds and rodents. They can eat up to 20 pounds (9 kg) of meat in a single meal. That's about the same as 160 hot dogs!

Once again, we did our best to follow the wild dogs as they raced through the thick brush. When we caught up with them again, the dogs were feasting on an impala. And now they had a lot of young pups with them. It was a very large pack, with maybe 15 or 20 members.

Doggie Bag

Have you ever brought home food from a restaurant in a doggie bag for a friend or family member? African wild dogs bring home food to share, too. It's for pack members that can't join the hunt, like pups and hurt or sick dogs. But the hunters don't use bags to carry the food—they use their stomachs. When the hunting team returns to the den after eating, they throw up the meat they swallowed. Then the other dogs gobble up the tasty "recycled" meal.

We drove toward the dogs and stopped a short distance away. They didn't seem to notice us. They just kept eating while we sat and watched. The guide turned off the vehicle, and we could hear a lot of yipping and crunching and chewing. The dogs shared with each other, and they let the puppies eat first.

Did You Know?

African wild dogs often play together before they hunt, yipping and yapping as if they're having a pep rally before a big game.

After the dogs finished eating, their bellies bulged and they rested in the shade. While the adult dogs slept, the pups played. It was just like my dogs did when they were puppies. The wild dog pups bit each other's ears and jumped on each other. They growled and pounced and kept interrupting the adults' nap time.

Joining the wild dogs' hunt was an amazing experience. I love looking back at the pictures I took that day. I have shots of the wild dogs when we first saw them near the tree. I have shots of them eating and chilling afterward. I don't have pictures of the most exciting moments of the hunt, but that's OK. I've learned that when you're photographing wild animals, there's no way you are in control of what your subject is going to do. It's not like a photo shoot, where you can tell the subject to do this or that. Try telling a wild dog to stop the hunt so you can take its picture! No, it doesn't work that way. You have to be ready when it's ready.

No matter what animal I saw on safari—click, click, click! I took lots of pictures, such as this one of a white rhino mother and baby.

CRUNCH TIME

This little baby white rhino is sticking close to its mother!

Chapter 1

TAGGING ALONG WITH RHINOS

The more time I spend with wild animals, the more I understand how much they need our help. On my safari trips, I've learned a lot about Africa's endangered animals, such as lions, wild dogs, elephants, and rhinos. Even some little animals, like some types of shrews, rabbits, and bats, are endangered.

Endangered means in danger of

going extinct. Extinct means none left! So it's "crunch time" for endangered animals. In basketball, crunch time is when you're behind in the game, and you've got to give it your all to win. But animals can't do it for themselves. Humans have to help.

Rhinos are one of the animals that need our help. I saw a white rhino on one of my first safaris. It walked heavily. The ground seemed to move when it jogged. It was a powerful moment for me.

Several years later, my friends and I tagged along on a conservation mission in South Africa with a wildlife veterinarian, or vet. Conservationists work to protect endangered plants and animals. They track and study animals in the field. On this trip, our job was to help the vet mark white rhinos' ears, so conservationists could track and count the animals.

The vet searched from a helicopter, while we drove through the bush in a vehicle. But it's not easy to find rhinos in the wild. They are very shy, and they blend into the scenery.

Did You Know?

A newborn baby white rhino weighs about 100 pounds (45 kg). It will stay with its mother for about three years.

The vet spotted one first. He called to say he had found a young white rhino grazing in the grass with its mother. He told us where it was, and we drove there.

As I watched from the ground, the vet lifted a dart gun. Then he shot a dart into the young rhino from the air. The dart held a drug that would make the rhino sleep.

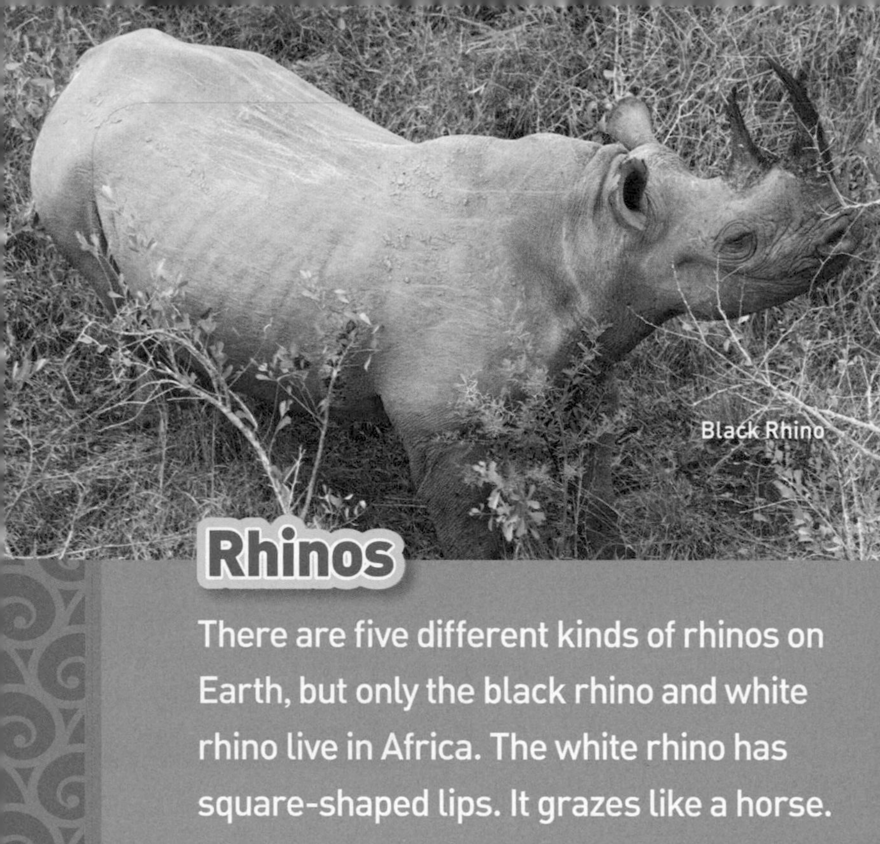

Black Rhino

Rhinos

There are five different kinds of rhinos on Earth, but only the black rhino and white rhino live in Africa. The white rhino has square-shaped lips. It grazes like a horse. It is the largest rhino. It can weigh as much as 6,600 pounds (3,000 kg). The pointy-lipped black rhino can weigh as much as 3,000 pounds (1,400 kg). It uses its upper lip to hook branches and leaves to eat, like a giraffe. Despite their names, both white and black rhinos are gray. Sadly, both are also very endangered.

The rhino was young, maybe a year old. It started running, and its mother ran along behind him. The first dart didn't work. The rhino just kept running, and his mother followed him. The vet shot a second dart. He shot a third. Finally, the little rhino slowed and dropped to the ground. The helicopter landed nearby. For a few minutes, I heard only the whoosh of the helicopter blades. Leaves and dust blew everywhere.

Now the team had to scare the mom away for a few minutes. Rhinos have poor eyesight, but they can hear well. So we made a lot of noise. The mother rhino ran off, but not too far.

Even though the young rhino was small, I could feel its power. His chest heaved. I touched his skin and felt him breathe. His skin felt like rough leather. To be so close to this amazing animal was a big deal to me. It made me so happy.

My friends and I helped the vet take a blood sample from the rhino. Then we helped pierce a small hole—about the size of the eraser on a pencil—in the animal's ear.

As we worked, I told the vet that I had never seen a black rhino. Black rhinos are smaller than white rhinos. They're also more aggressive. And black rhinos are harder to find than white rhinos. The vet asked if I wanted to ride in the helicopter. We could search for black rhinos. What do you think I said?

You're right. I wanted to go.

After we finished with the little white rhino, we watched him wake up and go back to his mother. Then I got into the helicopter. We flew over an area full of thick brush. The pilot said that's where black rhinos like to hide. Their skin is tough. They don't mind the thorns. And they feed on shrubs and branches there.

Suddenly, we saw a black rhino down below. He was browsing for food. When he heard our helicopter, he spun around in alarm. I lifted my camera and zoomed in. The rhino thumped the ground with his hooves. He moved his head, trying to scare us off. I thought, *We're pretty high in the air, rhino. You're not going to get us. But it was great to meet you.*

Even though I didn't speak her language, it was clear this tigress was telling us to scram!

Chapter 2

TIME-OUT WITH TIGERS

Every time I go on safari, I fall more in love with wild animals. I want to do more than just be a tourist. A few years ago, I met a National Geographic photographer named Steve Winter. He helped me see how powerful images can cause people to think, feel, and act. I wondered if I could help endangered species by sharing my photographs.

Steve invited me to go on a trip to India. He planned to take pictures of endangered Bengal (sounds like BEN-gull) tigers. Ten days later, I was on an airplane to India.

I love tigers. I love their stripes. I'm fascinated by how different they are from the big cats I've seen in Africa. I was excited about the trip.

Steve and I met up at the lodge at Bandhavgarh (sounds like BAND-uv-GAR) National Park. The first night, we talked about cameras and photography, and about how tough it is to see tigers in the wild. They are very shy animals. They have learned to stay away from humans. And their stripes help them blend in with their surroundings.

That night, I was so excited I couldn't

> **Did You Know?**
> From the tip of its tail to its nose, a male Bengal tiger can stretch nine feet (3 m)—that's almost as long as an NBA basketball hoop stands tall.

sleep. We got up early the next day and headed deep into the park in a vehicle. For two days, we looked for tigers from early in the morning until dusk. We saw a snake, deer, and a lot of monkeys, but no tigers. The monkeys played and made me laugh. The landscape was a lot greener than the places I had been in Africa. It was more like a forest.

On day three, I started to wonder if I was bad luck. We still hadn't seen any tigers. At one point, we searched for tigers on a dusty, deserted road. It was very hot. We stopped in the shade to wait at a water hole. Even though we hadn't seen a tiger, I felt lucky to spend time where tigers live.

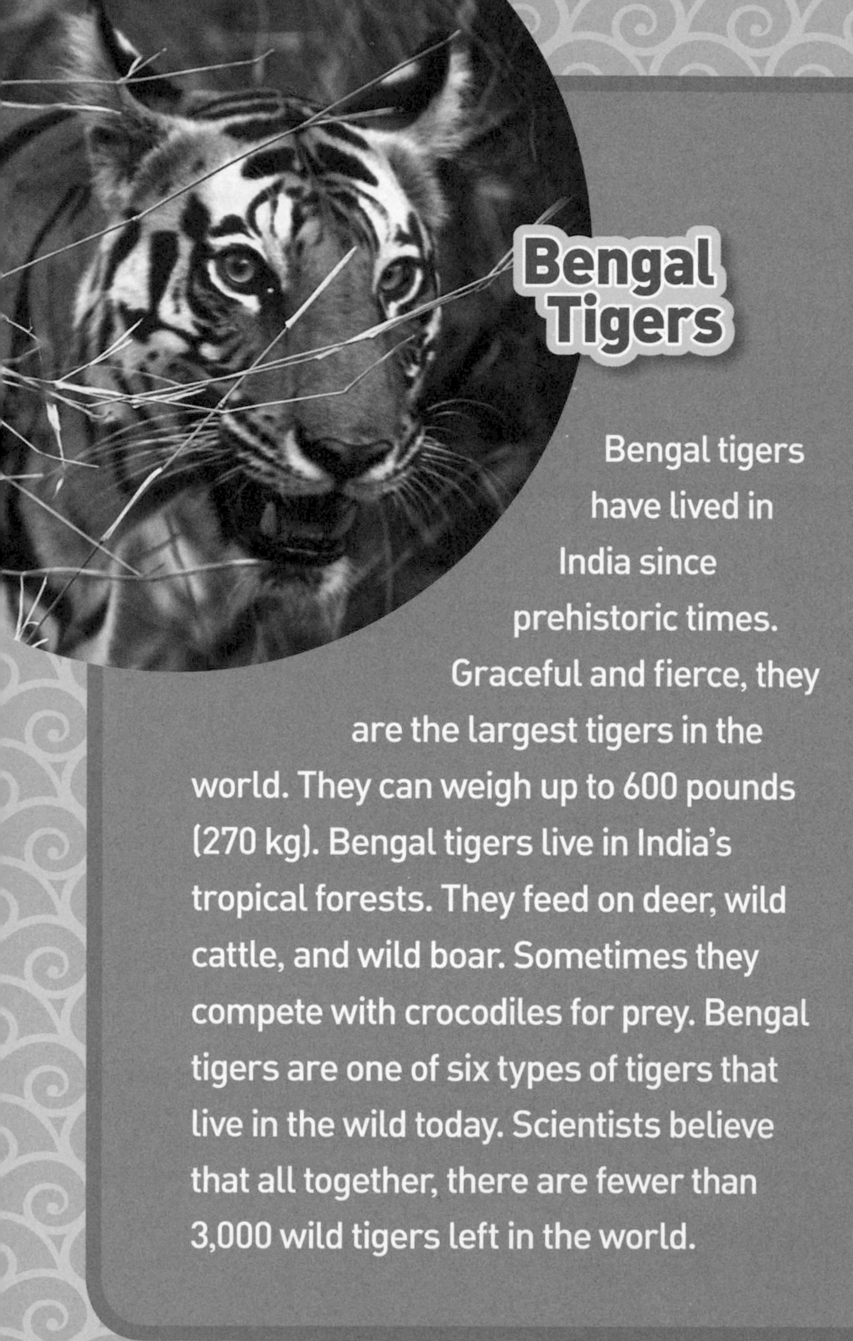

Bengal Tigers

Bengal tigers have lived in India since prehistoric times. Graceful and fierce, they are the largest tigers in the world. They can weigh up to 600 pounds (270 kg). Bengal tigers live in India's tropical forests. They feed on deer, wild cattle, and wild boar. Sometimes they compete with crocodiles for prey. Bengal tigers are one of six types of tigers that live in the wild today. Scientists believe that all together, there are fewer than 3,000 wild tigers left in the world.

Steve and I talked a lot about tigers while we sat there. I learned a lot. Tigers are the biggest and most powerful of the big cats. They are also the closest to extinction. But in India, Bengal tigers are experiencing a comeback.

We waited and waited and waited. After a while, I had pretty much given up.

But then all of a sudden, a female tiger stepped out of the bushes. She stared into my eyes. My heart just about stopped. Lions in Africa had never looked at me like that tigress did.

I took her picture. Then, boom! Here came two little cubs. They followed their mom closely. It was my first time seeing wild tigers. Maybe it was the cubs' first time seeing humans. After a while, the mom snarled. I think she was saying, "Yeah, don't follow us." Then she made a friendly chuffing noise to her cubs, and they left.

It's so hot in that part of India that the park closes in the middle of the day. But Steve and I were allowed to stay. We drove around all day in an open vehicle, and we set up camera traps. These cameras take pictures automatically. The motion of a tiger (or anything else) walking by triggers the camera. The animals take their own pictures, kind of how we take selfies.

To set up the camera traps, we checked out areas of the jungle where tigers like to go. We put one camera near a water hole where tigers go to swim and cool off. We put another in a tree that had lots of scratch marks. We could tell that tigers liked to leave their scratchy messages for each other on that tree. We angled the cameras just right to get the right shot. Some cameras sat high up in a tree looking down. Others looked up from a spot near the ground.

The place where we worked was so thick with plants that we couldn't see around us very well. A tiger could be hiding anywhere. Once, while we worked on setting up a camera, we heard monkeys screaming. Were they trying to warn us?

When the sun began to set, Steve and I headed out of the park. Later we learned that, right after we left, people in another vehicle had seen a huge tiger in the same spot! Our camera trap got a picture, too. I couldn't believe it. I wondered, *Had that tiger been watching us all along?*

It cracked me up when these cheetah cubs covered their mom's eyes like they were saying, "Nope, nothing going on here, Mom!"

Chapter 3

CHILLING WITH CHEETAHS

During the time I've spent on safari over the years, I've been lucky to see and photograph many amazing animals. My favorite place to go is Kruger National Park in South Africa. There's so much to discover there.

One time, my friends and I were out in a vehicle around sunset. We were looking for rhinos. But instead, we came across a family of cheetahs. We watched a mother and four cubs settling down in the tall grass for the night. When it got dark, we went back to the lodge. But early the next morning, we drove back to look for them again.

It was a good move. We got there just as the cheetah family was stretching and yawning and waking up. Then the cubs started to play at "attacking" their mother. They goofed around, play-fighting and chasing each other. I remember doing this with my brother when we were kids. We drove our mom crazy!

The cheetah cubs acted like they were hurting each other, just like Martin and I used to do. They practiced their offensive and defensive skills—just like basketball players! For cheetah cubs, it's how they learn to hunt and defend themselves.

I love cheetahs. Their speed is amazing. They can run in bursts up to 60 miles an hour (97 km/h)! That's as fast as a car on a highway. The cheetah is the fastest land mammal on Earth. Its long-legged body type is similar to the body type of a lot of basketball players. If only we could be as fast as cheetahs!

We watched the cubs play. I laughed when one cub covered its mother's eyes. It was like he was saying, "Hey Mom, don't look! My brother is doing something bad." The cubs were too funny.

Then the mom got tired. She put her paw out and stopped one cub mid-run.

It ran right into her paw. It was so cute.

The cheetah cubs gave us a lot of laughs that morning. But it's not all funny. Cheetahs are endangered, just like rhinos, lions, and tigers. I hope that some of my photos will make more people want to help save these amazing animals.

When I'm back on the court playing basketball, sometimes I think of the African wild dogs and other awesome animals that I've seen along the way. They've taught me a lot about the unselfishness and togetherness—and the fun—that come with being a successful team player. These animals have also taught me that Earth is not just our world. It's a privilege to share it with all the animals that live here, too.

Boris's Tips for Taking Great Pictures

Before my very first safari in South Africa, I got advice about photography from a friend who is a professional NBA photographer. She told me to always bring extra memory cards for my digital camera and to pack spare batteries. She showed me the basics and set me up so I could learn on my own. She also told me that photographing wild animals is a lot like shooting professional athletic games. You never know what's going to happen!

Here are some tips to improve your photography skills, like I did:

1. Experiment by taking pictures of different places, people, and things.
2. Practice by photographing your pets, animals at the zoo, or city scenes.
3. Don't always put the subject in the middle of the picture.
4. Take shots where the background is not too cluttered.
5. Focus on your shot and click two or three times, not 50 times.
6. Be patient. Your subject might surprise you!

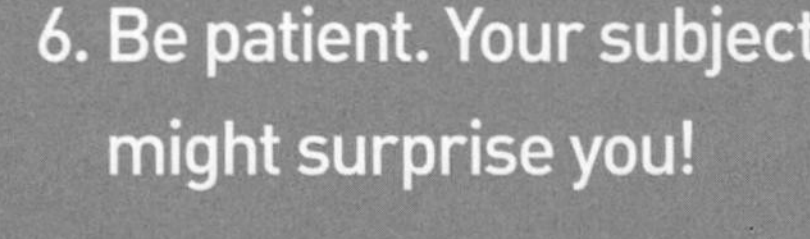

DON'T MISS!

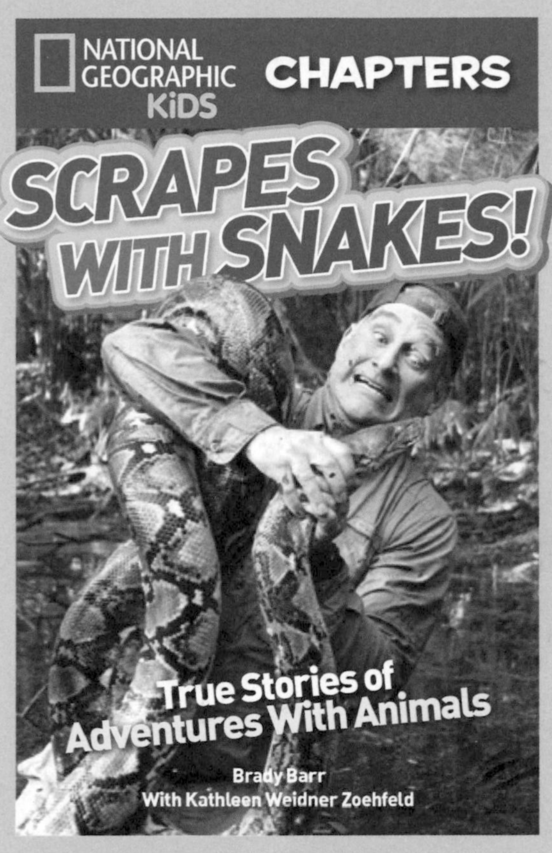

Turn the page for a sneak preview . . .

That's me, Brady Barr, with my friend Gerry Martin on the left. Together, we caught this giant Indian rock python.

The SNAKE That ATE COWS!

When catching a snake this big, it's always best to secure its head first. That's the biting end!

Chapter 1

SNAKE Problem!

I was waist-deep in water in a muddy swamp. I was trying not to think about the leeches that might be crawling up my legs. Then—I spotted it! Stretched out in front of me was the biggest snake I had ever seen. It looked as long as a bus!

What was I doing here? My name is Brady Barr. I'm a zoologist (sounds like zoh-AH-luh-gist), a scientist who studies animals. I've studied all kinds of animals all over the world. My favorites are reptiles—really big reptiles.

I've worked with some real giants. I've wrestled crocodiles over 18 feet (5.5 m) long. I've captured 10-foot (3-m)-long lizards and turtles the size of small cars.

But until that day in the swamp, I'd never come across a giant snake. Although they're among the biggest reptiles on the planet, they're very hard to find. And scientists know surprisingly little about them.

The swamp where I met the giant snake was in northern India. I was there with my friend Gerry Martin, a reptile expert. We had teamed up to study a rare and endangered crocodilian (sounds like krah-koh-DIL-ee-un). But our croc project soon took an unexpected turn.

Open Wide!

Some snakes can swallow things three times the size of their own head! How do they do it? Snakes have really flexible jaws. Human jaws are attached to the skull like a door on hinges. All we can do is open and shut them. A snake's lower jaw is not solidly attached at the chin, like ours is. Each side can move separately. A snake's jawbone is attached to the skull by stretchy bands of tissue, almost like rubber bands. Using its curved teeth to grip its prey, the snake can slowly stretch out its jaws and move its mouth around its meal.

When Gerry and I got to the small village near our research site, none of the people wanted to talk about crocs. All they wanted to talk about were snakes. They said they had a big problem. Their cows were disappearing. And they believed a giant snake was eating them.

Did You Know?

In *The Jungle Book*, by Rudyard Kipling, the giant, 100-year-old snake named Kaa is an Indian rock python.

Holy cow! I thought. *A cow-eating snake?*

This was a story we just *had* to look into. A snake large enough to eat a cow would have to be a true giant. We'd heard stories like this before. But no scientists had ever been able to check them out. Maybe this was our chance to prove those stories were true.

The villagers told us the giant snake

was eating their dogs, cats, and goats, too. They hoped maybe we could catch this snake and take it away to a safe place, far away from the village.

Gerry and I thought the snake was probably an Indian rock python. Rock pythons live in many different habitats. You can find them in low grasslands and on high mountain slopes. But the real giants usually stay near water.

The village was near the Geruwa (sounds like jeh-ROO-wah) River. Gerry wanted to go straight to the swampy area closest to the river, where the water was deepest. It was a great place for a big snake.

I really wanted to see this giant. But …

INDEX

Boldface indicates illustrations.

MORE INFORMATION

To find more information about the animal species featured in this book, check out these books, websites, and DVDs:

National Geographic Kids Everything Big Cats, by Elizabeth Carney, 2011

National Geographic Kids Mission: Elephant Rescue, by Ashlee Brown Blewett, 2014

National Geographic Kids Mission: Tiger Rescue, by Kitson Jazynka, 2015

National Geographic, "Animals: African Wild Dog," animals.nationalgeographic.com/animals/mammals/african-hunting-dog

National Geographic, "Animals: Hippopotamus," animals.nationalgeographic.com/animals/mammals/hippopotamus

National Geographic, "Animals: Leopard," animals.nationalgeographic.com/animals/mammals/leopard

National Geographic, "Big Cats Initiative," animals.nationalgeographic.com/animals/big-cats-initiative

Nat Geo WILD, *Hippo vs. Croc,* DVD, 2014

Nat Geo WILD, *A Wild Dog's Tale,* DVD, 2013

For all the conservationists who dedicate their lives to protecting and preserving the animal kingdom.
—B. D.

Dedicated to teachers like Michael Gueltig, who encourage kids to read about what they love.
—K. J.

CREDITS

All photography by Boris Diaw unless indicated below.
Cover: (Boris Diaw), Andy Lyons/Getty Images; Back Cover: Sam Forencich/NBAE/Getty Images; 4, Hugues Lawson-Body; 21, Lightboxx/Shutterstock; 21, belizar/Shutterstock; 21, Trombax/Shutterstock; 21, EcoPrint/Shutterstock; 21, Imnature/iStockphoto; 28, Elisabeth Riffiod; 42, Martin Diaw; 54, courtesy of Barry Gossage; 62, Cedric Beesley; 69, C. Robert Smith/National Geographic Creative; 70, Jullien Leleux; 73, Suzi Eszterhas/Minden Pictures; 96, Elisabeth Riffiod; 100, Hugues Lawson-Body; 101–107, photos courtesy Brady Barr

ACKNOWLEDGMENTS

Thanks to all my friends and family who came with me on these amazing safari adventures. Thanks to all the rangers and trackers who helped me experience India and the wild African way of life. Thanks to Catherine Steenkeste for introducing me to the art of photography. Thanks to Steve Winter for sharing a bit of his enormous experience with me. Thanks to Kitson Jazynka for rendering my stories so alive and colorful. Thanks to the editors of this book, Shelby Alinsky and Marfé Ferguson Delano, for appreciating what I can do outside of a basketball court. Thanks to National Geographic Kids book department and the National Geographic Society for showing the world the best of what nature has to offer. *—Boris Diaw*

A special thank you to: My husband, Guy, for all the amazing safari adventures we've shared in South Africa, and to our boys, Max and Quinn, who went on their first safari in 2014 and loved it as much as I do; Boris Diaw, for sharing hours of stories and laughs with me about his wildlife adventures in South Africa and India; all the wildlife conservationists around the world who devote their careers and their lives to saving wild animals; National Geographic Kids Books editor Shelby Alinsky and freelance project editor Marfé Ferguson Delano for entrusting me with this very special project. *—Kitson Jazynka*